Animals in Their Habitats

River Animals

Francine Galko

Heinemann Library
Chicago, Illinois

Designed by Ginkgo Creative
Printed and bound in the United States by Lake Book Manufacturing, Inc

07 06 05 04 03
10 9 8 7 6 5 4 3 2 1

Library of Congress Cataloging-in-Publication Data
Galko, Francine.
   River animals / Francine Galko.
      p. cm. -- (Animals in their habitats)
Includes bibliographical references (p.   ).
Summary: Explores the animals that make their habitat in rivers and streams.
   ISBN 1-4034-0183-7 (HC), 1-4034-0440-2 (Pbk.)
   1. Stream animals--Juvenile literature. 2. Rivers--Juvenile literature. [1. Stream animals. 2. Rivers.] I. Title.
   QL145 .G25 2002
   591.76'4--dc21
                    2001007659

Acknowledgments
The author and publishers are grateful to the following for permission to reproduce copyright material:
Cover photograph by D. Robert & Lorri Franz/Corbis
p. 4 Peter Miller/Photo Researchers, Inc.; p. 5 Peter Weimann/Animals Animals; p. 6 Eastcott/Momatiuk/Animals Animals; p. 7 Danielle Hayes/Bruce Coleman Inc.; p. 8 Rod Williams/Bruce Coleman Inc.; p. 9 McCutcheon/Visuals Unlimited; p. 10 Dwight Kuhn; p. 11 Richard Green/Photo Researchers, Inc.; p. 12 Roy Morsch/Bruce Coleman Inc.; p. 13 Pat and Ray Hagan/Bruce Coleman Inc.; p. 14 E. R. Degginger/Photo Researchers, Inc.; p. 15 Mark Smith/Photo Researchers, Inc.; p. 16 James Allen/Bruce Coleman Inc.; p. 17 Jack A. Barrie/Bruce Coleman Inc.; p. 18 Maslowski/Photo Researchers, Inc.; p. 19 J. Mitchell/OSF/Animals Animals; p. 20 Zig Leszczynski/Animals Animals; p. 21 A.H. Rider/Photo Researchers, Inc.; p. 22 Jeff Foott/Bruce Coleman Inc.; p. 23 Gary Schultz/Bruce Coleman Inc.; p. 24 Gary Meszaros/Visuals Unlimited; p. 25 Robert and Linda Mitchell; p. 26 Janis Burger/Bruce Coleman Inc.; p. 27 O.S.F./Animals Animals; p. 28 R. Toms OSF/Animals Animals; p. 29 Richard Day/Animals Animals
Every effort has been made to contact copyright holders of any material reproduced in this book.
Any omissions will be rectified in subsequent printings if notice is given to the publisher.

Some words are shown in bold, **like this.** You can find out what they mean by looking in the glossary.

To learn more about the otter on the cover, turn to page 16.

Contents

 # What Is a River?

A river is a kind of **habitat.** It is a stream of water. The water is always moving, mostly in one direction. The movement of water in one direction is called a **current.**

As water goes over hills or rocks, it might swirl or fly into the air. Sometimes, it moves against the current in circles or even backwards.

Where Are Rivers?

Rivers are all over the world. They often begin at lakes or ponds. The water moves from the lake or pond across the land.

Some rivers begin at **glaciers** on mountains. The water runs down the mountain as the snow melts.

 # River Homes

Rivers are full of animals. Musk turtles live in the water. But they come out to warm themselves in the sun.

8

Beavers build **lodges** on rivers. They cut down trees with their sharp teeth. They pull the trees into the river to build a home.

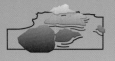 # Living on the River Bank

Belted kingfishers live on the **river bank**. They **burrow** in the mud to make nests. The mother bird brings fishes from the nearby river for the babies to eat.

Stoneflies begin life in the water, where they **hatch** from eggs. As adults, they live on rocks and trees beside the water. They eat water plants.

 # Living in the Water

Some rainbow trout live in cold rivers. They like the fast **current** and often come to the **surface** to find food.

Some manatees spend the winter in warm rivers. They do not like cold water. They eat grasses and plants in the water.

 # Living on the River Bottom

Some river animals live in the mud under the water. A softshell turtle will often **burrow** in the mud in shallow water. Then, it sticks its head out of the water.

Hellbender salamanders live on rocky river bottoms. They hide under rocks during the day. They eat crayfishes, snails, and worms.

 # Living in Moving Water

River otters spend most of their time in the water. They are good swimmers. Their **webbed** feet help them swim, even in moving water.

Harlequin ducks swim in rivers with fast **currents.** They dive to the bottom to catch **insects.** Sometimes, they use their strong **bills** to eat snails, crabs, and mussels.

 # Living Over the Water

Willow flycatchers build their nests in tall bushes and short trees. Sometimes, they live on islands in rivers. They eat a lot of **insects** while flying.

Ospreys often build their nests in tall trees near rivers or on islands in wide rivers. Some ospreys nest on large rocks in the middle of rivers!

 Finding Food in a River

Paddlefishes live on the muddy bottoms of rivers with slow **currents.** They eat very tiny plants and animals that live in the river.

Mergansers are ducks that swim under the water to catch fishes. The sides of a merganser's **bill** look like a saw. This helps them hold on to the fish.

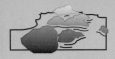 # River Predators

Some river animals are **predators.** They hunt other animals for food. The alligator gar is a fish. Its strong mouth can crush other fishes and small **mammals.**

Alaskan brown bears come to rivers to catch salmon. They swim in the water and fish. Then, they quickly eat the salmon.

Hiding in a River

Water dogs are salamanders that live on river bottoms. They usually have spots that help them blend in with the rocks. They like to hide under rocks and logs.

Harter's water snakes live in deep rivers with fast **currents.** They come onto the **river bank** to lie in the sun and hide under rocks.

 # River Babies

Mother salmon come to rivers to lay eggs. She lays eggs in a hole in the river bottom. After the eggs **hatch,** the young fishes look for **insects** and plants to eat.

Caddisfly **larvae** often live underwater or along the edge of a river. They make a net to catch small animals to eat from the moving water.

Protecting River Animals

Sometimes people put trash or **harmful chemicals** in rivers. Some companies put very hot water in rivers. Big boats that move fast make waves that crash into **river banks** and **erode** them.

28

These things harm river plants and animals.
Let's keep our rivers clean and protect
river animals from danger. When you visit
a river, put your trash in a garbage can.

# Glossary

bill mouth of a bird

burrow to dig

current movement of water in one direction down a river

erode to wear dirt away

glacier big piece of ice that slowly moves down a mountain or across land

habitat place where an animal lives

harmful chemical thing that can kill plants and animals

hatch to come out of an egg

insect small animal with six legs

larva (more than one are called larvae) very young insect

lodge beaver home

mammal animal, like humans, that has a backbone and hair or fur

predator animal that hunts and eats other animals

river bank land beside a river

surface top of a river or other body of water

web sheet of skin that fills the space between toes

More Books to Read

Ashwell, Miranda and Andy Owen. *Rivers.* Chicago: Heinemann Library, 1998.

Giesecke, Ernestine. *River Plants.* Chicago: Heinemann Library, 1999.

Robinson, Claire. *Bears.* Chicago: Heinemann Library, 1998.

Index